F.

by
J.B. Midgley

All booklets are published thanks to the
generous support of the members of the
Catholic Truth Society

CATHOLIC TRUTH SOCIETY
PUBLISHERS TO THE HOLY SEE

Contents

Acknowledgements

The CTS gratefully acknowledges recourse to the following resources:
The Penguin Dictionary of Saints, London, 1972; Butler's Lives of the
Saints, Ed. M.Walsh, Burns & Oates, Tunbridge Wells,1981; Oxford
Dictionary of Saints, D.H.Farmer, OUP, Oxford, 1978; The Lives of the
Fathers, Martyrs, and other Principal Saints, A.Butler, Virtue and Co.
Ltd., London, 1926; Vincent de Paul, Dr Peter Collet, Nancy, 1748 ;
Encyclopaedia of Catholicism, Harper and Collins, New York, 1995;
History of Christianity, O.Chadwick, Weidenfeld and Nicolson, London,
1995; The Divine Office, Collins, London, 1974; The Daily Missal,
Collins, London, 1982; The Roman Missal, Burns, Oates &
Washbourne, London, 1948; The Jerusalem Bible, Darton, Longman &
Todd, London, 1974; The Papacy, P.Johnson, Weidenfeld and
Nicholson, London, 1997; Book of Christian Quotations, T.Castle,
Hodder and Stoughton, London, 1982.

Man for all seasons

In some ways, the age in which Francis lived has similarities to our own. Then, as now, Europe was experiencing dramatic change, and the mind of the Church was necessarily focused on spiritual, intellectual, and institutional renewal: correcting aggressive heresy, reaffirming doctrine and practice, and preserving the ministerial priesthood that is at the heart of Catholic life. She continues to work for the revival of evangelism and the conversion of nations, withstanding secular assaults on faith, reversing the dilution of doctrine, and protecting the accessibility of the sacrifice of the Mass. In every season, the Barque of Peter navigates some stormy waters but, thankfully, there are Saints like Francis de Sales whose eager and powerful intercession does not diminish with the passing of time.

God, in His kindness, provides every season with holy men and women to encourage His people, and that the Holy Spirit breathes an impetus to refresh faith, doctrine, religious leadership, and energy in the mission Christ delegated to His Church. Francis is a luminous example of the local Apostle who preserves and teaches the Faith received from the Twelve personally appointed by Our Lord. As Bishop, his priorities were to preach the Gospel, preside at Mass, care for the clergy, and ensure that spiritual centres of liturgical and cultural excellence stimulate hope and the practice of the Faith. He helped his flock understand that prayer opens the mind to God's word, and respond to his desire that everyone plays a part in His plan of salvation through a personal conception of His Son. Indeed Francis truly was "a fascinating figure, so balanced, courageous, sensible, devout, another 'man for all seasons'".

I should like to thank Fr John Daley, I.C. for guiding a renewed appreciation of this remarkable man.

Downham Market, Easter 2008.

Early years and education

The world awaiting Francis

The Reformation in Europe had divided Catholics and
Protestants. From 1562 to 1598, France suffered from the
resultant civil hostilities remembered as the "Wars of
Religion". However, the cause of these was not so much
the difference in religion as the sudden and violent death
of the French king, Henry II, in 1559 that left the country
without a leader and at the mercy of contending barons.
Furthermore, when it suited political purposes, Catholic
France was just as likely to invade Catholic Italy as
Protestant Germany or Switzerland.

On 3rd December 1563, Pope Pius IV had at last been
able to confirm the decrees of the Council of Trent thanks
to his nephew, Saint Charles Borromeo, who had skilfully
managed to assemble the 255 representatives for the final
session. As a platform for 'Counter-Reformation', the
Council sought moral reform and an affirmation of
traditional Catholic doctrine and devotion. Heresy was
corrected, the teaching on original sin clarified, and the
permanence of marriage emphasised. Unjust taxation and
the sale of Indulgences were forbidden, clerical
concubinage condemned, and bishops brought under

much needed control. The central beliefs that had been rejected by the Protestant reformers were re-defined, classified, and have remained characteristic of Catholic expression ever since.

Birth

Four years later, Count Francis de Boisy of Sales and his wife Frances of Sionas were living in the family's ancestral Chateau of Sales in Savoy near Thorens. This was a mountain village thirty miles west of Mont Blanc and twenty south of Geneva in the diocese of Annecy. They had dedicated one room in their home to Saint Francis of Assisi and had mounted a picture of him preaching to the birds and fishes. Here on 21st August 1567, two months earlier than expected, Countess Frances gave birth to a baby boy for whom the portrayed Saint would be a life-long patron. The next day the baby was baptised in Thorens parish church and christened with the name Francis Bonaventura. His early arrival in the world was to leave him delicate as a child, but he would recover to be a handsome, energetic man of great charm who inspired universal affection and admiration.

Both parents were devout, but it was the gifted Countess Frances who would be the major influence in his development. She inspired in her little boy a respect for the Church, a love of prayer and a holy way of life, and introduced him to the lives of the Saints that she sensibly adapted to suit his age. He went with her whenever she made charitable visits, and helped to distribute food, clothing, and alms to the poor. He saved some of his own food on their behalf and, if he had nothing to give, begged his relatives to make a contribution.

Francis was but an innocent five year old when the infamous Saint Bartholomew's Day Massacre took place on 24th August 1572, the Feast of the Apostle. Admiral Coligny, a leading Protestant, was in Paris for the wedding of the Protestant Henry of Navarre to Marguerite, the Catholic sister of Charles IX, then ruling France. When an attempt was made to assassinate Coligny, Charles panicked and, at the instigation of his mother Catherine de Medici, ordered the slaughter of all Protestants in Paris. On this shameful occasion, twenty thousand victims died including Coligny.

Schooling

Not long after this terrible event, Countess Frances asked an exemplary priest, Father Deage, to help her conduct her son's early education and be the tutor and guardian of his formative years. After a year's initiation to learning, both parents agreed the time was right for wider experience, and Francis became a pupil at the nearby school at Rockville as a preparation for enrolment in the college in Annecy. Here, in 1575, he made his First Holy

Communion and received the Sacrament of Confirmation in the Dominican church.

He was an able and industrious student, with a keen mind, a retentive memory, sound judgment and, as he did more than was strictly required, made excellent progress with the happy knack of not arousing resentment. He remained fascinated and inspired by the lives of the saints and, with maturing piety, the intention to dedicate his life to the service of God and his people grew within him. When he was eleven, he received the tonsure with the grudging permission of his father, Count Francis, who hoped that his eldest son and future head of the family, would have a brilliant career in the world. However, he found some comfort in the fact that this was not an irrevocable renunciation of the world.

University

The University of Paris, with its 54 constituent colleges, was one of the great centres of learning. In 1581, when Francis was 14, his father said he should enter Navarre College, an institution traditionally favoured by the sons of Savoyard nobility. Francis was hesitant, correctly assuming that the ethos and customs would scarcely be compatible with his vocation, so he persuaded the Count to let him seek admission to Clermont College that was directed by the Jesuits, and known for its religious atmosphere and academic excellence.

Accompanied by Father Deage, he duly found accommodation near the college at the Rose Blanche hotel in the Rue Saint-Jaques. He studied Greek and Hebrew, made rapid progress in rhetoric and philosophy, and showed particular aptitude in theology. To please his father, he also took courses in riding, fencing, and dancing - without much enthusiasm it must be said, since he was more concerned with serving God and his neighbour, with prayer, and studying the Scriptures. However, the skills acquired contributed to the development of the savoir faire, social grace, and genuine charm that captivated others throughout his life.

Illness and spiritual growth

Not everything came easily. Francis was overtaken by a painful period of spiritual dryness and sense of being abandoned, a depression that lasted until he made an appeal to Our Lady that resulted in a return of confidence and peace of mind. He was befriended by Father Angelus who, before becoming a Capuchin friar, was a duke and a former marshal of France. He taught Francis not to be discouraged by weakness but to overcome the Devil's temptation to be despondent by prayer, mortification, and works of mercy. Francis added wearing a hair shirt three days a week to the acts of self-denial he already practised, made a perpetual vow of chastity in the church of Saint Stephen des Grez, and placed himself under the special protection of the blessed Virgin.

After four years, still watched over by the faithful Father Deage, Francis transferred to the University of Padua to study Law. Father Poisssevin, of the Society of Jesus, became his spiritual director and guided his continued theological studies, especially the 'Summa Theologiae' of Saint Thomas Aquinas. He also introduced him to the 'Spiritual Exercises' of Saint Ignatius that was to have permanent influence in his life with its pattern of meditations, examination of conscience, forms of prayer, contemplation of God's forgiveness, and the place of Our Lord's life, passion, and resurrection in the divine plan.

In the light of the Ignatian exercises, Francis decided to compose a rule of life for himself that displayed a constant awareness of God's presence, and the habit of relying on his help in every action and enterprise. At one point during his time in Padua, he fell victim to an illness that threatened his life, so much so that a tearful Father Deage asked him what he wanted to do about his funeral. "Nothing", Francis answered cheerfully, "unless my body be given to the anatomy theatre to be dissected. It will be of comfort if I can be of some use dead, having been none while alive." He recovered, to the great relief of all who loved him.

First appointment

After graduating as a Doctor of Law, he toured Italy visiting Saint Charles Borromeo's great cathedral in Milan, and the House of the Holy Family in Loreto. He was moved to tears at the tombs of the Martyrs, but was less impressed by the worldly grandeur of Rome and other historic cities. He rejoined his family at their lakeside home of Chateau Thuille just outside Annecy. By now his father had obtained from the Duke of Savoy an appointment for him as counsellor of the Chamberry Parliament. Francis had so far mentioned his desire to be a priest only to his mother and his cousin, Canon Louis de Sales; but the time had now come when his father must be told. It so happened that the Provost of the Geneva Chapter had died recently and, without Francis knowing, Canon Louis used his influence to arrange his appointment to the vacancy with the hope that this would soften paternal opposition. The plan worked: Count Francis gave his blessing. Francis immediately adopted ecclesiastical dress and assumed his position.

Deacon

Almost immediately, Bishop Claud de Granier of Geneva ordained him Deacon and commissioned him to preach. Francis believed that this important ministry required him to be a man of prayer, and consequently prepared his sermons as much before the crucifix as in preparatory research. His sermons were instantly effective and eagerly awaited, his listeners commenting that, "He delivered the Word of God with a mixture of majesty and modesty in a strong, sweet voice, with an animated

manner of gesture but without vanity or affectation."
What attracted them most was the sincere humility with
which he spoke from the heart.

Ordained priest

After a preparatory period of intense personal devotion,
Francis, now 26, was ordained priest on 18th December
1593, and took up his duties with an apostolic ardour that
was never to leave him. He celebrated Mass early each
morning, heard confessions and preached. He then set off
into the rural areas to instruct and bring solace to the
villagers, especially the many whose lives were harsh and
poverty-stricken as a result of civil conflict. He tried to
avoid applause and approval for anything he did, wanting
only to please God and advance His glory. However he
could not prevent his piety, charity to the poor, care of the
sick and those in prison, from endearing him to everyone.
Before the first anniversary of his priestly ordination, he
had founded at Annecy the Confraternity of the Holy
Cross whose members committed themselves to teaching
catechism, comforting the sick and those in prison and,
by mediation and reconciliation, preventing law-suits that
he considered to be incompatible with Christian charity.

The Geneva mission

John Calvin, a French lawyer, humanist and Biblical commentator (1509-1564) who had died three years before Francis was born, had studied for the priesthood before being attracted to Protestantism. He contended that the Church needed restoration to his perception of her original purity, and went to Geneva to promote the idea of a Christian state. His treatise, 'Institutions of the Christian Tradition', expressed the principles of 'Calvinism', and these are worth recording because they illustrate the magnitude of a mission that would soon be entrusted to Francis de Sales.

Calvinism

Calvin taught that the Old and New Testaments are the necessary and sufficient source for understanding the Christian Faith; God is the absolute Sovereign whose will determines everything for human salvation; and the Fall destroyed free will and all the actions of a depraved humanity are therefore sinful; Faith is sufficient to ensure justification and salvation; Christ's atonement is only for the elect because God has pre-ordained those to be saved or damned; and because his grace is irresistible, the elect have no choice but to do his will; the Mass is idolatrous, and that the New Testament makes no mention of a Catholic, clerical hierarchy that must therefore give way to the Biblical offices of deacon, elder, presbyter; teacher, and pastor.

Calvin's Geneva community flourished and won many adherents throughout France. Between 1559 and 1561, Calvinist pastors increased the number of 'Reformed Churches' to 2,000 that attracted about ten percent of the entire population, a phenomenon that disturbed spiritual and secular authorities alike. Catherine de Medici and her husband Henry II mounted a fierce pursuit of these Protestants who were taking possession of Catholic churches, their policy inciting rebellion, a call to arms, and many deaths. In 1560, some Protestant nobles had tried to kidnap Francis II, Catherine's eldest son and husband of Mary Queen of Scots, and this is why French Protestants became known as Huguenots (from the Genevan *eiguenotz*, meaning conspirators or confederates).

First missionary work

The faith of Catholics of the Chablais on Lake Geneva's southern shore had been particularly assailed and, in 1594, Duke Charles Emmanuel of Savoy asked Bishop de Granier to appoint missionaries to bring his subjects back to the Church. When the Bishop summoned his Chapter and outlined the very real hazards and difficulties, only Francis de Sales had the courage to volunteer, and the Bishop accepted his offer eagerly. Friends and relatives did their utmost to dissuade him from what they saw as dangerous folly, but their tears and warnings, his mother's anxiety, and his father's active opposition did not deter him.

On 14th September, the feast of the Exaltation of the Holy Cross, he set out to win back the Chablais, accompanied only by his doughty cousin, Canon Louis. When they arrived at the Chablais frontier, they sent back their horses and walked the rest of the way on foot so that they could arrive in the manner that our Lord had recommended to Apostles. When they reached the capital Thonon, they found only seven people who acknowledged they were Catholics but, fortunately, the commander and garrison of the castle of Allingens still held fast to the Faith and offered them accommodation.

Every day the intrepid missionaries worked and preached in Thonon and the neighbouring villages, constantly braving physical abuse and threats from heretics. Francis had several miraculous escapes from assassins, intent on killing him and once had to spend a night in a tree because a pack of wolves decided to pursue him. At first there were few signs of progress and the Count often wrote to his son pleading with him to come home for the sake of his mother, but Francis was determined to win hearts and minds. In the face of hardship and persecution, he composed leaflets that presented and explained Catholic teaching, and laboriously copied them by hand for wide distribution. These were later to form the volume of his 'Controversies'.

The fruits

Francis' perseverance was blessed and began to bear fruit about 1597. Unexpectedly, his first converts were among the military who not only returned to the Faith but also abandoned their habits of swearing, dueling and drunkenness. Then the harvest wonderfully increased in villages and towns, so much so that the Bishop sent Jesuits and Capuchins from Annecy to continue and expand the good work under Francis' direction. Conversions became more and more frequent, and there was a steady stream of the previously half-hearted and lapsed who wanted to be reconciled to the Church. Astonishingly, even many leading Calvinists embraced the Faith, and they claimed it was Francis' meekness, approachability, and refusal to condemn, that accounted for the thousands of conversions he had brought about. His theory was that "Whoever preaches with love, preaches effectively". He certainly achieved a remarkable recovery and transformation in four years, and even greater blessings were to come the following year.

Catholic practice returns

The fierce religious conflict that had been sparked by the Saint Bartholomew's Day Massacre was alleviated by Henry of Navarre's accession as Henry IV of France in 1598. He immediately became a Catholic, famously observing that 'Paris is worth a Mass'. He showed tolerance to the Huguenots, and in the Edict of Nantes, promised to protect them from oppression. That tension did not disappear overnight is exemplified by the Duke of Savoy's abortive attempt to banish Calvinism from the Chablais, but at least the practice of Catholicism was officially restored. When Bishop de Granier made a pastoral visit to Geneva, he received a warm welcome and was in awe at the results of self-sacrifice and tireless zeal on the part of Francis and his co-workers. He was able to administer the Sacrament of Confirmation, and even presided at the 'Forty Hours' devotion when the Blessed Sacrament is exposed: opportunities that had been previously unthinkable in Thonon.

Over the next few months, Francis who was now 31, regained possession of the parishes and churches that had been seized by the heretics. He organised new ones, appointed zealous parish priests and, to his great joy, was able to celebrate the Mass of the Nativity on Christmas Day 1598. His endeavours had won acclaim as far as Rome, and people everywhere sought his spiritual direction. This presented no threat to his humility as he continued to undertake the least enviable tasks, with continued delight to be among the poor, the suffering, and the marginalised.

Bishop and Shepherd

When Francis visited Annecy in 1599, Bishop de Granier proposed his appointment as coadjutor bishop with right of succession to the diocese of Geneva, though this would require approval from the Holy See. He was reluctant at first, but eventually yielded to his Bishop's insistence and in submission to what he accepted as the will of God. He then succumbed to a fever, the more dangerous because he was physically worn out and anxious about future responsibilities, but his indomitable spirit soon brought recovery. He was called to Rome to be examined by Pope Clement VIII and, among others, the Jesuit Cardinal Saint Robert Bellarmine and Saint Charles Borromeo's cousin, Cardinal Frederick Borromeo. It was a searching interview, but he answered questions with a simple modesty that did not disguise his erudition, expertise and saintly qualities. His appointment as Geneva coadjutor was confirmed.

Loreto and Paris

Towards the end of the year, Francis made another devotional visit to the Holy Family's House at Loreto on his way back to Annecy. He arrived in time to support his father during the last hours of his final illness and comfort him with the Sacraments. Despite the sadness of loss, he took up his duties with characteristic energy, and his preaching during Lent resulted in an identifiable resurgence of fervent devotion and fidelity. A few months later, Diocesan business took him to Paris where he charmed every level of society and received the warmest approbation. The Lenten sermons he preached to the royal Court in the chapel of the Louvre were inspirational and his continued evangelism brought many Calvinists and other wandering sheep back to the Church.

The visit gave him opportunity to help the future Cardinal, Pierre de Berulle (1575-1629), establish the French Congregation of the Oratory that was modelled on that of Saint Philip Neri. He also smoothed the paths for the Carmelites, recently reformed by Saints Theresa of Avila and John of the Cross, to settle in France. King Henry was among the many who consulted him on matters of conscience, and he offered Francis an enviable pension to stay and be bishop of the first diocese to become vacant. Francis thanked the king but told him that God wanted him to be bishop in Geneva, and there he must stay to the end.

New mission as bishop

When Bishop de Granier died in Autumn 1602, Francis went into retreat for three weeks to prepare for his own consecration. Following the example of Saint Charles Borromeo, he revised his plan of life according to new circumstances, and this he implemented as soon as he became Bishop of Geneva on 3rd December 1602 at the early age of 35. He remained ever faithful to his rule that he should wear only coarse wool and never silk; that the bishop's residence should have simple furnishings with any paintings only of a devotional theme; that he would always visit on foot and avoid coaches; his household would have only two priests, one as his chaplain and the other to attend to the running of the establishment; there would be no lavish meals; and he would personally attend the feasts of devotion in the town's churches, preach to the people, encourage them, and take every opportunity to visit the sick and poor.

Daily routine

It became his habit to get up at 4:00 every morning to meditate, say the Divine Office with his clergy, and read from the scriptures before celebrating Mass at 7:00am. After Mass and thanksgiving, he attended to diocesan matters until lunch that was followed by conversation before administration and correspondence were resumed and concluded with prayer. After the evening meal and congenial conversation with his brother-priests and household staff, he read to them from a suitable book until it was time for Evening Prayer and Matins. He fasted on Fridays, Saturdays, and the vigils of Our Lady's feasts, and continued to wear his hair shirt and use the discipline.

However, he refrained from ostentatious penance because he maintained that fidelity in fulfilling the ordinary demands of life to which one was called, and interior self-denial, were the highest form of mortification.

Loving shepherd

Francis immediately embarked on an extensive and demanding programme of diocesan visitations, reforming religious houses where necessary en route. Where things had to be put right it was with a lightness of touch that did not destroy confidence and, where efforts were admirable, they were praised and encouraged. He published a new liturgical Ritual, and inaugurated a series of ecclesiastical conferences for instruction and the dissemination of best practice. He organised the teaching of catechism on Sundays and feast days throughout the diocese, taking the Annecy classes himself with such enthusiasm that the 'Bishop's Catechism' was vividly remembered long after his death, and remained an example for all parish priests. Wherever he went, he recommended the habit of recalling the presence of God when the clock struck the hour by making the Sign of the Cross and reflecting for a moment on Our Lord's passion.

He never begrudged time and effort in associating with the people entrusted to his care, especially those who might be considered the less important. In public and personal contacts he is described as "always patient with impeccable good manners, warmly sensitive to others' feelings with a genuine interest in their well-being, merciful in judgment, clear in expression, dignified, approachable, and modest." Of himself he merely said, "I have to be Bishop of Geneva in public, but I am Francis de Sales in private." Before he ordained candidates for the priesthood, he made sure they possessed the qualities essential to their calling and had been properly prepared - a message that encouraged any who may have become lukewarm. His concern for the French language, Science, and the Arts spurred him to found the Florimontane Academy at Annecy, anticipating the French Academy by 30 years.

Francis' thoughts were always for the poor, the suffering, and the misguided. He made some horrendous journeys to help those who had been overtaken by natural disasters, and effectively brought their needs to the attention of landowners and appropriate authorities. People were in awe at his selfless charity, humility, and gentleness, not least in the Confessional where he saw sins as thorns that hurt the soul, and had to be extracted carefully so as not to cause more pain, though he was properly firm when kindness did not work.

Fame and reputation

In 1604, the Duke of Savoy, in response to requests from of his subjects, invited Francis to preach the Lenten sermons in Dijon. These bore such wonderful fruit among the people that King Henry wanted to keep him at the realm's centre. He offered him an abbey with its lucrative revenues, and told him he had already spoken to Pope Clement who would willingly create him a Cardinal. With a charm that prevented ever giving offence or hinting at ingratitude, Francis declined, saying that he dreaded wealth, and was singularly unsuitable for dignified titles. The King in admiration commented, "The Bishop of Geneva, by the happy independence in which his virtue has placed him, is as far above me as I, by royal coincidence, am above my subjects."

The following Lent, he was invited to Chamberry, but his great delight was in preaching in small villages, mingling with the people and being able to exercise his care for the poor. On one occasion his forthright housekeeper took him to task for giving away the contents of the larder; he confessed: "You're right. I am an incorrigible creature and, what is worse it looks as if I shall long continue to be so." Glancing towards the Crucifix he added, "How can we deny anything to a God who reduced himself to this condition for the love of us?"

Advising the Pope

Pope Paul V was elected in 1605 and, perhaps harshly, is remembered more for censuring Galileo's statement that the earth revolves round the sun, than for his promotion of Church reforms and the encouragement of the worldwide missions. He asked Francis to help settle a dispute that had arisen between the Dominicans and Jesuits concerning the teachings on God's grace. Francis advised the neutral stance he always favoured when scholastic opinions were put forward. He felt that to do otherwise could offend charity and squander time that could be better spent honouring God. In 1609, he went to Bellay to consecrate as bishop the eminent French priest John Paul Camus who became a life-long friend and author of *The Spirit of Francis de Sales*.

Acclaimed author

The *Introduction to the Devout Life*, is based on letters that Francis sent to his cousin Madame de Chamoisy, in which he shows that Christian devotion has its place in secular life as much as in the cloister while we prepare for eternal joy. When the universal application and appeal of his guidance led to publication in 1609, it was greeted as a spiritual masterpiece, and Archbishop Villars of Vienna wrote to the author, "Your book charms, inflames, puts me in raptures, as often as I open any part of it", and other commendations led to translation in other languages. King Henry and his queen, Mary de Medici, sent a jewel-adorned copy to James I of England who was so impressed by the contents that he asked, "Why none of my bishops can write with such feeling and unction."

John Wesley, the founder of the Methodist movement, was another who said that it was a great and salutary work. However, not all was sweetness and light, and Francis had his critics. He was accused by some who should have known better of condoning "gallantry and flirtation, dancing, comedies, and unseemly jests." One fierce critic publicly denounced the book during a sermon, and burned it in the pulpit. Hurtful though such ignorant opposition was, Francis did not allow his peace of soul to be disturbed.

The informal treatise *The Love of God* is the story of the love for God that is instinct in human hearts and lives. To share this sublime subject with others, to console and encourage them, Francis paints a picture of his own soul that experiences the sentiments of divine love, its state of fervour and sensible consolation, and also the opposite in dryness, trials, suffering, and darkness. Again, King James received a copy, and was so moved by what he read that he asked to see the author. When Francis heard this he said, "Give me the wings of a dove, and I will fly to the king, into that great island, formerly the country of saints, but now overwhelmed by the darkness of error. If the Duke permits, I will arise and go to that great Nineveh; I will speak to the king and announce to him, with the hazard of my life, the word of the Lord." The Duke of Savoy was reluctant to let Francis accept invitations to preach even in French cities lest he be lured away and, for the same reason refused permission with the added motive on this occasion that he did not want to appear subservient to another ruler. Other writings include *Preparation for Mass*, *Instructions for Confessors*, and *The Standard of the Cross* in which Francis responded to Calvinist attacks on Catholic reverence for the instrument of our salvation.

The Order of the Visitation

In 1604 Francis was preaching the Lenten sermons in Dijon, and it was here that he met Jane Frances de Chantal (1572-1641). She came from a noble Burgundian family and had taken a vow of chastity after being tragically widowed when she was only 29. There was immediate rapport and in response to her request, he willingly advised her on her duties as daughter, mother and member of society, eventually becoming her spiritual director from whose wisdom she benefited while he lived. At Annecy in 1607, she shared with him her thoughts about entering the religious life.

Jane Francis de Chantal

She had been much impressed by the mystical wisdom of Saint John of the Cross and Saint Theresa of Avila to which she had been introduced by the holy Carmelite nun, Anne of Jesus; she found the same wise realism in Francis who encouraged her sense of vocation. They both recognised what they called 'the squalor of the Cross' in the squalor of towns and cities, and determined to do something about it. They recruited a number of helpers including Francis' cousin Madame de Charmoisy whom he urged to "become a servant of the poor, serve them when they are sick with your own hands, cook for them at your own expense, do they sewing and washing." Jane Frances herself took "her scissors and medicine into dens and hovels, cropped infested hair, dressed ulcers, and cleaned the incontinent."

From such work evolved the decision to found a new religious congregation that would enable women, including those in delicate health, to lead the religious life and at the same time work outside the cloister. This was a departure from the norm of enclosure that would later be followed by Saint Vincent de Paul when he founded the Sisters of Charity. In 1610, Francis opened the first convent of a dozen nuns at Annecy with Jane as superior, but the Holy See insisted that enclosure and separation from the world must be observed, a decision that led to the vocation becoming contemplative in character.

Rule

Francis had chosen the Rule of Saint Augustine for the new community because it demanded few corporal austerities. He told the Sisters that humility before God and meekness before one's neighbour are more important than austerity, and that perfect self-denial is in obedience. About meekness he wrote to them: "If there was anything more excellent than meekness, God would certainly have told us. There is nothing to which he so earnestly exhorts us as to learn of him and be 'meek and humble of heart'. Surely it is right to obey this command of Our Lord and learn from him the virtue he so eminently practised and so highly esteems. No one is better informed in these matters than God himself." The Rule allowed the sharing of goods in common, so that there would be no time-consuming or fruitless worries about the necessities of life, though it advocated detachment from possessions in the spirit of poverty that relinquishes ownership or right to use.

Spirituality

Francis pointed them to the Mother of God's spirit of piety, charity, humility, meekness and simplicity, and promoted the daily recitation of the Little Office of the Blessed Virgin Mary that Alcuin of York had composed in the ninth century, and Saint Peter Damian revised in the eleventh. He introduced them to the methods of meditation, and the shorter recollections that focus inward attention on the presence of God with the thought that words and actions can affect spiritual life, and explained the essential benefits of spiritual reading and retreats. Pope Paul V raised the congregation to the status of an Order that was blessed with rapid expansion thanks to the prudence and dedication of the Founders.

War and unrest

In 1555, at the Peace of Augsburg, the Catholic German empire had accepted the legality of the Protestant religion in Lutheran states. However, in 1618, as the Order of the

Visitation blossomed, hostilities were resumed when some Bohemian nobles threw two of Emperor Ferdinand's regents out of a fatally high window in Prague. Ferdinand declared war on Frederick V, the Protestant king of Bohemia, seized Protestant territories, and closed Lutheran churches and schools in Bohemia, Austria and Moravia. The conflict engulfed Europe as Lutheran rulers in Germany and Denmark tried to reclaim territories with the assistance of English and Dutch forces.

Denominational disputes, and the impetus of the Catholic Counter-Reformation became a cloak for nationalist causes and secular ambition and some strange alliances, as much political as religious, were forged. Catholic France joined forces with Protestant Sweden, and several Protestant German states aligned themselves with the Emperor. Throughout Europe, innocent men, women, and children were slaughtered by invading armies and foreign mercenaries, or left to starve as their villages and crops were laid waste. It would not be until 1648 that the Peace of Westphalia would restore to each ruler in the Empire the right to determine the religion of his state, and Calvinism, Lutheranism, and Catholicism were all declared legitimate.

Vincent and Louise

In 1619, Francis and Jane Frances went to Paris to inaugurate the Order's convent in the city and, by happy coincidence, met Saint Vincent de Paul. There was an immediate union of holy minds, and it is a measure of the esteem in which they held him that they entrusted him with the spiritual care of the Visitation Sisters. Vincent described Jane as one of the holiest people he had ever met, and he brought Francis' original intention of an unenclosed Order to fruition when he founded the Sisters of Charity with Saint Louise de Marillac That the two great men were friends gave an added stimulus in their assisting Pierre de Berulle to refresh the spiritual life if the Church in France.

They made telling contributions to the French School of Spirituality that motivated Catholic revival in France and her immediate neighbours; it remained an exemplary influence in the universal Church until the twentieth century.

Twilight years

Francis preached in Grenoble throughout Lent 1617, and was so successful "with his usual conquest of souls and the conversion of many Calvinists", that they invited him again the following year. Ever the realist however, he recognised that the unremitting workload, and fostering the Order of the Visitation, were taking toll on his health, and he decided to appoint a coadjutor. In consultation with Cardinal Archbishop Frederick Borromeo of Milan, who had approved his own appointment as Geneva coadjutor back in 1598, he chose his brother John Francis de Sales who was duly consecrated Bishop of Chalcedon at Turin in 1618.

Sought after

Typically, he remained as busy as ever. In 1619, he went to Paris to negotiate the marriage of Louis XIII's daughter Christina of France to the Prince of Piedmont. When he had concluded arrangements to the satisfaction of all parties, the Princess asked him if he would be her spiritual director, and he agreed but only on condition that he remained in his diocese of Geneva. Nonetheless, Cardinal Henry de Gondi, Archbishop of Paris, invited him to be his coadjutor with right of succession, but he

was adamant that he should remain where God had given
him responsibility. The next Lent, he preached in Saint-
Andre-des-Arc where the congregations were so large
that distinguished prelates and nobles who came to hear
him struggled to find a space in the pews.

Generous dedication

His learning, eloquent sermons, the conferences he held,
his invariably engaging conversation, and his manifest
holiness of life moved not only the devout but also
heretics, unbelievers, and those who had strayed from the
path of moral principles. Particularly noticeable was the
tenderness with which he welcomed wanderers back to the
fold: "Come my dear children, let me embrace you, let me
hide you in the bottom of my heart. God and I will assist
you; all I ask of you is not to despair. I shall do the rest."

His genuine affection extended even to their temporal
needs and his purse was as open to them as his heart. To
those who said he was too indulgent to sinners he asked,
"Are they not part of my flock? Has not Our Blessed
Lord given them His blood, and shall I refuse them my
tears? These wolves will be changed into lambs, and the
day will come when, cleansed from their sins, they will
be more precious in the sight of God than we are. If Saul
had been cast off, we would never have had a Saint Paul."

Bishop Camus of Bellay pleaded with Francis not to
preach twice every morning and evening for the sake of

his health, but he responded with a smile "that it cost him less to preach a sermon than to find an excuse not to do so when invited, that God had appointed him as a pastor and preacher, and everyone must follow their calling." He added, "But I am surprised that people flock so eagerly to hear me, for my tongue is slow and heavy, my conceptions low and my discourses flat, as you are witness." When he returned to Annecy, the demanding routine of preaching, teaching, and hearing Confessions continued unabated. When one of the frequent plagues broke out, he did nothing to protect himself as he tended to his flock, always with joyful trust in Providence. He told friends, "My heart desires to be sacrificed to the pure and holy love of my Saviour. It is good to love, to labour, to rejoice only in God."

Good and faithful servant

In 1622 the Duke of Savoy asked Francis to accompany him to Avignon to visit Louis XIII who had just returned from successfully resolving the civil war in Languedoc. Although not well enough for a long winter journey, he agreed because he wanted to discuss the needs of the French section of his diocese with the King. He must have sensed that life was drawing to a close because he put all his affairs in order before leaving and, to their dismay and anxiety, said good-bye to everyone as if he had no expectation of seeing them again. When he reached

Avignon, he followed his usual disciplined routine and, because he was praying the Divine Office, was not even tempted to look out of the window to witness the King's triumphant procession passing by. When he and the Cardinal of Savoy went on to Lyons to attend the King, he declined the luxurious apartment prepared for him, preferring to lodge in the gardener's cottage in the grounds of the Visitation Convent of Bellecour.

No matter where he went it was impossible to avoid the burdens of fame. Crowds wanted to see him, seek his advice, listen to him, hear their confessions, and every religious house asked him to come and preach to them. After a month, he badly needed a rest, but did not spare himself for the good of souls. During a bitterly cold Advent, he said he was glad to share hardship and poverty that the Holy Family experienced. He continued to preach, administer, and refuse nothing that was asked of him, though he was painfully embarrassed by the marks of honour and invitations that poured from the King and the nobility.

Final illness

It was with joyful serenity and gratitude that he participated fully in the Christmas Liturgy but, in the evening of 27th December, the feast of Saint John the Evangelist, he fell gravely ill with what has been described as a paralytic seizure or apoplexy. He received the Last Sacraments, but not the Viaticum of Holy Communion since he had celebrated Mass that morning.

Well-meaning physicians, anxious to prolong a treasured life, attempted some drastic remedies that included the application of poultices so hot they scorched the skin. Francis had recovered consciousness sufficiently to feel the intense pain but did not complain, only murmuring, "My heart and my flesh rejoice in my living God; I will sing the mercies of the Lord to all eternity. When shall I appear before his face? Show me my beloved where thou feedest, where thou restest at noonday? O Lord, my desire is before thee and my sighs are not hidden from thee. My God and my all! My desire is that of the eternal hills."

As the agony continued, he prayed, "Wash me O Lord from my iniquities and cleanse me from my sin," and comforted those around him, "Weep not for me my children; the will of God must be done". When they suggested offering Saint Martin's prayer "If I am still necessary for Thy people, I refuse not to labour," he was distressed by being compared to a Saint and said he was an unprofitable servant whom neither God nor the people needed. His humble and confident trust in God's mercy was still evident as his condition worsened, and he breathed his last contentedly at 8.00pm on the feast of the Holy Innocents, 18th December 1622. He was still only fifty five.

Legacy

A leading Calvinist who heard that Francis had died said: "If we honoured any man as a saint, I know none more worthy than this man since the days of the Apostles". Francis' body was embalmed, escorted with reverent honour to Annecy where he had asked to be buried, and laid to rest in a splendid tomb near the high altar in the church of the first convent of his Order of the Visitation. His heart was enshrined first in a wooden reliquary in the Church of the Visitation at Lyons, and later exposed in one of gold donated by Louis XIII. Within a short space of time the miracles that God had worked through him while he was alive, were augmented by many more reported and verified through his intercession. These included the resuscitation of two people who had drowned and cures of some who were blind or paralysed. Cardinal Fabio Chigi, who became Pope Alexander VII thirty years later, Louis XIII, and Louis XIV were among those who attributed their recovery from illness to his patronage.

Jane Frances de Chantal outlived her guide and collaborator by 19 years. In 1628, when there was a severe outbreak of the plague, she organised the convent in Annecy to care for the afflicted, and charmingly prevailed on the authorities to provide for the sick and bereaved. At the same time, her personal life was saddened by a succession of family deaths, but her resolve was undiminished as, for the next 13 years, she made systematic pastoral visits to all the convents of her Order, nurturing growth, religious observance, and the context in which the Sisters could best achieve the aims of their vocation. She died in 1641 on a return journey from Paris, was canonised in 1767 by Pope Clement XIII, and her feast is 12th December.

In 1662, Pope Alexander raised Francis to the honours of the altar in the first beatification to be celebrated in Saint Peter's Basilica in Rome and, when he canonised him three years later, he established his Feast on January 29th, the anniversary of his funeral at Annecy. He was declared a Doctor of the Church by Pope Pius IX in 1877 and his relics were translated to a splendid new shrine at Annecy in 1912. He was nominated the patron of writers, editors, and journalists by Pope Benedict XV in 1923. Since the revision of the Roman Calendar in 1969, the Feast of Saint Francis de Sales is 24th January.

Devotion and writings

There can be no better comment on Francis' story than what he says himself. He has always attracted a special affection and reverence for the spiritual direction and support he gave to clergy and laity through conversations, sermons, letters, and treatises and, above all, by his example. He had a sensitive perception of the needs of the Church, and the relevance of her tradition and teaching in every circumstance. In the light of Our Lord's humanity, he explained that life's routine can be holy without the need for heroic gestures, that "religious devotion does not destroy, but perfects" and, given nature's limitations, that "the human mind is so constructed that it resists vigour and yields to gentleness". He admitted his own "hasty and impetuous temper" that he controlled by doing all he could to emulate Our Lord who was "meek and humble of heart" and, in this way, tried "to steer a predominant inclination towards a virtue that also saves the trouble of pretending to be other than we are."

He guided souls to self-sacrifice and love of God with gentleness, advised them about friendship, behaviour, language, dress, recreation, and fidelity in all things great and small, and in the joyful hope of fulfilment in sharing Our Lord's resurrection and glory.

He explained that humility is recognisable only in acts of charity, and warned against impetuosity, heroic gestures, and severe austerity. A favourite saying was that more flies are caught with a spoonful of honey than a barrel of vinegar, but he left no one in doubt about the rigour of his ideals, the requirements of Church teaching, and Christian responsibilities.

Even a brief selection from his major works, *The Introduction to the Devout Life* and the *Treatise on the Love of God*, draws us closer to a Saint and Doctor of the Church whose life is a light for all seasons.

Universal audience

My intention is to instruct those who live in towns, in households, at the court and, by reason of their circumstances, lead an ordinary life. In creation, God commanded the plants to bring forth their fruit each after its own kind: even so, he commands Christians who are the living plants of his Church, to bring forth fruits of devotion, each one according to his kind and vocation.

Christian living

We must prepare ourselves to confront departures from God's law with great care and diligence, and rest assured, that as many victories as we gain, so many precious stones will be placed in the crown of glory which he is preparing for us in heaven.

Trust in God

In all you do, rely completely on God's providence.
Imitate little children who hold fast to their father with
one hand, and with the other gather strawberries or
blackberries along the hedgerows. So too, as you gather
and handle the goods of this world with one hand, you
must with the other hold fast to the hand of your heavenly
Father, turning yourself towards him from time to time to
see if your actions or occupations please him. Above all,
take heed that you never leave his hand, or think to gather
more, or to gain some advantage. Should you be parted,
you will not be able to go a step further without falling to
the ground.

We may walk with God in the steps of our own will
that we conform to His, with our obedient hand always
holding the hand of the divine intention, and following it
wherever it leads. On other occasions we may walk with
Our Saviour without any will of our own, simply letting
ourselves be carried by his good pleasure, a kind of
consent that can be called unity of our heart with God's.
We do not produce the effects of this will of good
pleasure. They proceed from his providence, but they
happen to us.

Our will can no more die than our soul, yet sometimes
it reaches beyond its limits to live totally in the divine
will. This is when it neither wills nor cares to want

anything at all, but gives itself to divine providence. It so immerses itself in this good pleasure that it is seen no more and is hidden with Jesus Christ in God.

The Eucharist

The sacrifice of the Mass is the highest and greatest act of worship that one can give to God, so much so that one single Mass surpasses the honour and glory that can be given him for ever by the angels, the saints and the blessed Virgin Mary.

The Eucharist is the most sacred of all devotions, the holy and sacred sacrifice, the heart of the Christian religion. It is an ineffable mystery which embraces the untold depths of divine love, and in which God gives himself, freely bestowing all his blessings and graces on us. When prayer is united to this divine sacrifice it has indescribable power and, with the priest, you may offer the sacrifice of your Redeemer to God his Father on your own behalf and that of the whole Church. What a privilege it is to be united in so blessed and mighty an action.

When you receive Holy Communion, your first intention should be to advance, strengthen, and comfort yourself in the love of God. You must receive with love that which love alone has caused to be given to you. If people ask you why you receive Holy Communion frequently, tell them it is to learn to love God, be purified of imperfections, delivered from misery, comforted in affliction, and supported in weakness. Tell them that because you are imperfect, weak, and sick you need to communicate often with him who is your perfection, strength, and physician.

Prayer

Prayer brings the mind into the brightness of divine light and the will to the warmth of divine love: nothing else so purges the mind of ignorance, and the will of wrong inclinations. It is a fountain that revives our good desires and causes them to bring forth fruit. It washes away the stains of our weaknesses and clams the passions of the heart.

Above all, I recommend the prayer of the heart in meditating on the life and passion of Our Lord. Then, your soul will be filled with him, you will learn his expression, and frame your actions according to his example. he is the light of the world and, through him and for him, we are enlightened and illuminated. If we remain close to him and heed his words, we shall learn to speak, to act, and to will like him.

It is a mistake to think that prayer can effect perfection without perseverance and obedience. Though perseverance does not come from our power, it certainly comes within our power...God's will is as much in sickness as in health, and we can therefore make sickness itself a prayer.

Accustom your self to pass from prayer to action: the merchant to business, the married woman to her household and family, with gentleness and tranquility so that the spirit is not disturbed. Prayer and action are both according to God's will, and we must make passage from one to the other in humble devotion.

Preaching

The sermons I like best are those that have more love for one's neighbour than indignation against him. If possible, avoid showing any sign of displeasure when you are preaching, or at least anger, as I did one day when they rang the bell before I had finished! The test of a preacher is that his congregation goes away saying, not "What a lovely sermon!", but "I will do something".

Love of the poor

If you love the poor, go among them frequently, take pleasure in bringing them round you, and in visiting them and conversing with them willingly. Mingle with them in the church, in the street, and elsewhere. Be straightforward with them, speaking with them as their friend. But also let your hands be rich, giving to them freely of your abundance. Would you want to go further than that? If so, do not stop at being poor with the poor, but make yourself poorer than they are. Become the servant of the poor; go and help them when they are sick, feed them, serve them, minister to them.

Turning to God

I do not approve of those who begin to reform a person with external things - hair, face, or dress. We must begin from within because God asks "Turn to me with your whole heart, give me your heart," because the heart is the mainspring of our actions. So, Our Lord says, "Set me a seal upon your heart," for whoever has Jesus Christ in his heart will soon show it in all his outward actions. If he is in your heart, he will also be in all your gestures, your eyes, your mouth, your hands, so that you can say with Saint Paul, "It is no longer I who live, but Christ who lives in me."

True Devotion

According to the state of life, the practice of devotion differs for the gentleman and the artisan, the servant and the prince, for widow, young girl or wife, and is adapted to their particular strength, circumstances and duties. Is the solitary life of a Carthusian suited to a bishop? Should those who are married practise the poverty of a Capuchin? If workmen were to spend as much time in church as religious, if religious were exposed to the same pastoral calls as a bishop, such devotion would be ridiculous and cause intolerable disorder.

True devotion never causes harm, but rather perfects everything we do; a devotion that conflicts with anyone's state of life is undoubtedly false. The bee sucks honey from the flowers without injuring them, leaving them as whole and fresh as when it found them. Devotion goes further; not only is it harmless to any state of life, it adorns and blesses it. Precious stones of all kinds when steeped in honey become more brilliant thereby, each one according to its colour; so everyone becomes more lovable and more perfect in his vocation if he combines it with devotion. It makes the care of family peaceful, the love of husband and wife more sincere, the service of one's king more faithful, and every task more pleasant and a joy.

It is a mistake to think that life in the army, the workshop, the court, or the home is incompatible with devotion. Purely contemplative, monastic or religious devotion cannot be practised in these callings; yet these are not the only kinds of devotion; there are many others suitable for those who live in the world and capable of leading them to perfection. Wherever we find ourselves we not only may, but should, seek perfection.

Christ, the object of devotion

Consider our Saviour who, in his humanity, looks from heaven upon everyone in the world. Use the imagination to see the Saviour in his humanity as though he was nearby. Let us be happy to serve him in his kitchen and in his pantry, to be his lackeys, porters and chambermaids ... If you wish to meditate upon our Saviour on the cross, imagine yourself to be on Mount Calvary, or that the crucifixion is happening in the very place where you are ... In God's eternal present moment we can keep close to the Saviour in meditation, observe his words, actions and affections and then, we shall with the help of his grace, learn to speak, to act, and to will like him.

Consideration for others

In my opinion, it is a greater virtue to eat what is served, whether you like it or not, than to choose the worst. Then you renounce both your own taste and choice in an unpretentious mortification that inconveniences no one, and is appropriate to life in the world.

Exterior cleanliness reflects interior probity, and propriety is determined by time, age, condition, company, and occasion. Let there be nothing about you that fits badly, but an attempt to look beautiful is a foolishness to be tolerated only in youth.

Patience

The virtue of patience is the one that most assures us of perfection. Be patient with everyone, but above all with yourself. I mean, do not be disturbed because of your imperfections, and always rise up bravely after a fall. He

who is so fretted by his own failings will not correct
them; all profitable correction comes from a calm,
peaceful mind. In the spiritual life, it is right that you
should begin again every day, and never think that you
have done enough.

Holiness

All of us can attain to Christian virtue and holiness, no
matter in what condition of life we live, and no matter
what our life-work may be. One of the best intentions we
can have in all our actions is to do them because Our
Lord did them.

A vigorous and constant soul can live in the world
without receiving any worldly taint; can find springs of
sweet piety in the midst of the briny waters of the world.

The truly loving heart loves God's good pleasure not
only in consolations but, and especially, in afflictions also.

Let us belong to God even in the thick of the
disturbance stirred up round about us by the diversity of
human affairs. True virtue is not always nourished in
external calm any more than good fish are always found
in stagnant waters. It will be quite enough to receive the
evils that come upon us from time to time, without
anticipating them by the imagination.

The height of love's ecstasy is to have our will not in
its own contentment but in God's ... To live according to
the spirit is to think, speak and act according to the

virtues that are in the spirit and not according to the sense
and sentiments which are in the flesh. O my soul, since
you are capable of God, woe to you if you content your
self with anything less than God.

Answering God's call

A good vocation is simply a firm and constant will in
which the called person serves Almighty God in the way
and in the places in which he has called him. We must not
be unjust and require from ourselves what is not in
ourselves ... God requires a faithful fulfillment of the
merest trifle given us to do, rather than the most ardent
aspiration to things to which we are not called. Great
works may not always lie in our way, but every moment
we may do little ones excellently, that is, with great love.

Free will

We have freedom to do good or evil; yet to make choice
of evil is not to use, but to abuse our freedom. They are
blessed who do not their own will on earth, for God will
do it in heaven above... Faith fills a man with love for
the beauty of its truth, with faith in the truth if its beauty.

Relationships

To love our neighbour in charity is to love God in man.
... Nothing is so strong as gentleness; nothing as gentle
as real strength... There was never an angry man that

thought his anger unjust... Make yourself a seller when you are buying, and a buyer when you are selling, and then you will sell and buy justly.

Our words are a faithful index of the state of our souls...Try as hard as you like but, in the end, only the language of the heart can ever reach another heart; while mere words, as they slip from your tongue, do not get past your listener's ear. The kindling power of our words must not come from outward show but from within, not from oratory but straight from the heart.

Be at peace regarding what is said or done in conversations; for if good, you have something to praise God for, and if bad, something in which to serve God by turning your heart away from it... The business of finding fault is very easy; that of doing better very difficult... Half an hour's listening is essential except when you are very busy. Then a full hour is needed.

To reflect on all our ordinary actions by a continual self-examination would be to tangle ourselves in a labyrinth from which we could never be extricated... Drones make more noise than bees but all they produce is wax not honey. Those who torment themselves with eagerness and anxiety do little, and that badly.

From the Liturgy

Dear Lord, it is your will that, for the salvation of souls, your blessed bishop and confessor Francis became all things to all men. Grant that we too may be filled with the sweetness of your love and, with his wise guidance and merits to support us, we may come to everlasting happiness. (*Collect*, Roman Missal, 29th January 1948).

Father, you gave Francis de Sales the spirit of compassion to befriend all men on the way to salvation. By his example lead us to show gentle love in the service of all. (*Daily Missal*, 24th January 1982).

Jesus said to His disciples, 'As the Father has loved me, so I have loved you. Remain in my love... This is my commandment: love one another as I have loved you...You are my friends if you do what I command you' (*Jn* 15:9-17). (From the Gospel for the Feast).

The Spirit of Francis de Sales

Succeeding generations are grateful for the devotion with which his friend, Bishop Camus recorded the Saint's own words and deeds. For those seeking holiness, there is the continued inspiration of his meekness of heart, and shining personality that is absorbed in God with overflowing of divine love. A few examples are offered.

"Truth must always be charitable because zeal that is bitter does more harm than good. Reprehension can be a food that is hard to digest and ought to be so carefully prepared on a burning fire of charity that all harshness evaporates. Otherwise, like unripe fruit, griping will result."

"Charity does not seek itself or its own interests, but only the honour and interests of God. Pride, vanity and passion cause bitterness and harshness. A wise silence is always better than a truth spoken without charity, and a remedy that is applied injudiciously can turn to poison."

"In speaking of meekness, his favoured and ambitioned virtue, Francis said he had spent years studying it in the school of Jesus Christ and was still disappointed by his lack of progress. He was often put to the test during very busy times, and when crowds of people bringing their needs and problems scarcely gave him time to breathe. He explained, 'God makes use of these occasions to see if our hearts are strong enough to withstand attack. I have promised my heart and my tongue that I will confine them to the bounds of duty, and I look on the crowds who come to see me as children who run to their Father's embrace. The hen does not refuse her little ones protection when they gather round her but extends her wings to cover them. So too, my heart must expand in proportion to the numbers of poor people who come to see me.'"

"The person who possesses Christian meekness is affectionate and tender to everyone. He is disposed to forgive and excuse the frailties of others, and the goodness of his heart appears in an affability that influences his words and actions, and sees everything in the most charitable light. He never utters a harsh word, is never rude or haughty. His serene countenance distinguishes him from the violent and the angry who know only how to refuse, or give way with a bad grace and so lose all merit."

"The best remedy against sudden impatience is friendly silence. No matter how little one speaks, self love is bound to claim a share and a word can escape that disturbs peace and harmony. If nothing is said and one stays cheerful, the storm passes, anger and indiscretion take flight, and pure, lasting joy remains."

The Society of Saint Francis de Sales (Salesians)

A remarkable sign of devotion to Saint Francis de Sales has been given by Saint John Bosco, 1815-1858, who dedicated his life to the education of boys and young men, assisting in their material needs, and attending to their religious instruction. In 1859, with the help of similarly disposed priests, he established a "pious society" to develop this ministry throughout Italy, and placed it under the special protection of the Saint whose pastoral and apostolic spirit had so inspired him. Many of those educated by the worldwide Salesians have entered the priesthood and the religious life.

Vincent de Paul

Amid the wars and turmoil of 16th-century Reformation France, and in the midst of great suffering and poverty, Providence provided an amazing example of apostolic zeal. Highly intelligent, physically small, and burning with love for Christ in the poor, Vincent de Paul stimulated a major change in the social consciousness of France and far beyond. His Religious Orders for men and women continue today. This account of his life and times captures the amazing spirit of this humble and courageous man, who truly loved and served the poor.

Barry Midgley, a retired Headmaster, has spent most of his professional life in Catholic education. He has published several titles with CTS and lives in East Anglia.

ISBN: 978 1 86082 503 3

CTS Code: B 701

A world of Catholic reading
at your fingertips ...

CTS

... now online
Browse 500 titles at

www.cts-online.org.uk

Catholic Faith, Life, and Truth for all